Here's what people have to say about the Jannah Jewels Adventure Book Series:

*I can't continue without saying it one more time: Powerful Young Muslim Girls! No damsels in distress, no dominating male protagonist, no cliché girly nonsense! ... This is exactly what our girls need to grow up reading.*
–Emma Apple, author of best-selling 'Children's First Questions' Series

*Learning about Islamic history and famous Muslims of the past makes these books a historical book lover's wish, and the Islamic twist is a plus for young Muslim readers. Jannah Jewels has been Muslimommy approved as kid-friendly!*
-Zakiyya Osman, MusliMommy.com

*I love all of the Jannah Jewels books, and the fact that you combine history and adventure in your stories. I also liked that you put the holy verses of Quran that remind us to stay close to Allah and I liked the fact that in one book you mentioned the verse from Quran which mentions the benefit of being kind to your enemy. I have read all of the Jannah Jewels books and even read two of these books in one day, that's how much I like these books!*
–Fatima Bint Saifurrehman, 8 Years Old

*I could really feel the love that went into this book – the characters, the places, the history, and the things that the author clearly strongly believes in and wants to share with our children and the wider world through her heroines...My daughter's verdict? "I would give the book a 10 out of 10 mum"*
–Umm Salihah, HappyMuslimah.com Blog

*Fantastic book! My child was turning pages and couldn't wait to read the next chapter. So much so he's as' for the next book in the series.*
-Mrs. S. A. Khanom, Book Revie

D1225427

*This was a great book with a nice story. I am happy to say that all three of my daughters (ages 13, 8 & 6) fell in love with it and can't wait for the next installment. My daughters could relate to the characters and have read the book several times.*
–Jessica Colon, Book Reviewer

*It's wonderful to see young Muslim women defined for who they are, their strengths and talents, and not for what's on their head.*
–Kirstin, Woodturtle Blog

*My kids liked the characters because they are modest in their mannerisms and dress, so that was something my daughter could relate to. Even though the characters are girls, it had enough excitement and the presence of supporting male characters to be read by both girls and boys. Throughout the book there was an essence of Islamic values and there was a lot of adventure to keep us guessing!*
-HomeStudyMama, Book Reviewer

*So inspirational... The young girls in these series are defined by the strength of their character. These non-stereotyped female role models are what our girls (& boys) need to read about. The storyline is engaging and subtly teaches moral lessons. Highly recommend these books.*
-Amn, Book Reviewer

*It's important for girls and boys, Muslim and not, to have strong, non-stereotyped female role models. Jannah jewels bring that in a unique way with a twist on time travel, fantasy, super heroes and factual Muslim history. It is beautifully written, engaging and an absolute must for any Muslim (and non-Muslim) kids library! My daughter LOVES The Jannah Jewels...*
–Hani, Book Reviewer

*We've reviewed 100s of Islamic non-fiction and fiction books from every single continent, except Antarctica, and none of the fiction books have made such an impression on our family as Jannah Jewels.*
–Ponn M. Sabra, Best-selling author, AmericanMuslimMom.com

# By Umm Nura

Vancouver

*This book is dedicated to my three little Jannah Jewels.*

*May your roots sink deeply into the rich soil of God's love.*

Published by Gentle Breeze Books, Vancouver, B.C., Canada

Copyright 2014 by Umm Nura
Illustrations by Nayzak Al-Hilali

Visit us on the Web! www.JannahJewels.com

ISBN: 978-0-9867208-6-4

November 2014

# Contents

**Sport:**

Archery

**Role:**

Guides and leads the girls

**Superpower:**

Intense sight and
spiritual insight

**Fear:**

Spiders

**Special Gadget:**

Ancient Compass

**Carries**:

Bow and Arrow, Ancient
Map, Compass

HIDAYAH

**Sport:**

Skateboarding

**Role:**

Artist, Racer

**Superpower:**

Fast racer on foot or
skateboard

**Fear:**

Hunger (She's always
hungry!)

**Special Gadget:**

Time Travel Watch

**Carries:**

Skateboard, Sketchpad,
Pencil, Watch

JAIDE

**Sport:**

Horseback Riding

**Role:**

Walking Encyclopedia, Horseback Rider

**Superpower:**

Communicates with animals

**Fear:**

Heights

**Special Gadget:**

*Book of Knowledge*

**Carries:**

*Book of Knowledge*, has horse named "Spirit"

**IMAN**

**SARA**

**Sport:**

Swimming

**Role:**

Environmentalist, Swimmer

**Superpower:**

Breathes underwater for a long time

**Fear:**

Drowning

**Special Gadget:**

Metal Ball

**Carries:**

Sunscreen, Water canteen, Metal Ball

# SUPPORTING CHARACTERS

JAFFAR

JASMIN

MOE

SLIM

# THE JANNAH JEWELS ADVENTURE 4:

## CORDOBA, SPAIN

ARTIFACT 4: A VIAL OF SECRET SUBSTANCE

*"When you serve the elders, you receive blessings in your life."*
~Master Archer to Student

Assalamu alaykum dear Reader,

What beautiful wisdom was shown by the Jannah Jewels in the last adventure in Baghdad. Jaide learned a valuable lesson in sacrifice by giving up her Artist pen even though she loved it so much. The mission is becoming more challenging for the Jannah Jewels, while Jaffar and his friends get stronger.

In this next story, the Jannah Jewels will need your help to solve the mystery of the missing artifact. This time there are special instructions and if they are not carefully followed, the Jannah Jewels might be stuck back in time forever.

Come along, dear Reader, let's help Hidayah, Iman, Jaide and Sara to collect the missing clues and solve the Secrets in Spain.

Adventure Awaits!

With warmest salaam,
Umm Nura

# Prologue

Long ago, there was a famous archer who mastered the way of the Bow and Arrow. He was given the enormous task of protecting the world from evil. He was a peaceful archer, who knew an important secret that made him extremely powerful - not only in archery but also in other ways you would not believe. The secret was written inside a scroll, placed in a box, and locked away inside a giant Golden Clock to be protected from the hands of evil.

But the Master Archer was growing old, and the time had come to pass on his duty to an apprentice. He watched his students carefully every day. The students trained extra hard to earn the Master Archer's approval. Two students caught the Master Archer's eye: Khan and Layla. Khan was fierce in his fights, made swift strategies and had strong hands. Layla was flawless in her aim, light on her feet and had intense vision. Khan wanted to be the next Master Archer more than anything in the world. Layla, on the other hand, just wanted peace in the world, no matter who became the next Master Archer.

Finally, the day dawned when a new Master had to emerge. Despite everyone's surprise and for the first time in history, the duty was given to a girl—Layla. Layla trained relentlessly and over time proved her just and peaceful nature. The Master Archer said, "It is only the humble, the peaceful and those who can control their anger that are allowed to possess the secrets of the bow and arrow."

Before long, Khan and Layla were married and practiced the way of the Bow and Arrow together. In time, they had two children, a boy named Jaffar and a girl named Jasmin.

Jaffar grew up to be a curious and gentle spirit who loved to practice calligraphy, read books, and sit for long hours under shaded trees. Jasmin, on the other hand, liked to play sports, tumble in the grass, and copy her mother in archery. They all lived peacefully together in a villa in the old walled city of Fez in Morocco, *or so it seemed*.

Khan fought with Jaffar, his son, every day, urging him to work harder at archery. Had it been up to Jaffar, he would simply have sat for hours reading his books and practicing calligraphy. He was just not interested in archery, but his father was so fierce that Jaffar had no choice but to practice with his sister, Jasmin, who was a natural. As the days went on, trouble brewed, and gloom and misery settled upon the villa's walls. Over time, Jaffar grew to be an outstanding archer, fierce and powerful, much like his father, despite his not wanting to do so, and soon forgot all about his reading and writing. On the other hand, Layla practiced archery differently. She practiced to refine her skills and herself; she never used archery for fighting, but for strength-building and purifying her heart. Soon, this difference in practicing the Bow and Arrow caused problems for everyone.

*   *   *   *

Far away in Vancouver, Canada, Hidayah was sitting in her classroom, bored as usual. She had always thought that nothing exciting ever happened, but this day everything was about to change. Some days ago, as Hidayah walked home from school, she had spotted a mysterious woman in the neighbourhood park. The woman was wearing dark red, flowing robes, and something behind her sparkled in the sunlight. It looked as though she were moving into the empty house on the hill. No one had ever lived there for as long as Hidayah could remember.

Now, Hidayah decided she was done with being bored. That afternoon, as soon as the school bell rang, Hidayah started the long trek up to the house on the hill. At the top of the hill, she huffed up the porch stairs and tiptoeing, peeked into one of the windows. She couldn't believe what she saw! It was the woman in long, dark red, flowing robes with a bow and arrow in her hands, standing so completely still that she looked like a wax statue. Her strong hands were wrapped around the bow, and her eyes were intently gazing at the target across the room. She was so focused and still that Hidayah had to hold her breath for fear of making any sound. Hidayah sat mesmerized, waiting for the woman to let go of the arrow. *But she did not let go.*

So it happened that, day after day, Hidayah would hurry up the hill to watch this mysterious woman. And everyday she came closer and closer to the door of the house. Several months went by in this way until one day, Hidayah finally mustered enough courage to sit on the doorstep. To her amazement, the door was wide open. Hidayah thought she had not been noticed. Then, for the first time, the woman let go of the arrow, which landed in a perfect spot right in the centre of the target. The archer turned and said, "So, you have come." She looked right into Hidayah's eyes as though she was looking through her. Hidayah, at first startled, regained her calmness and with her head lowered said, "My name is Hidayah, may I be your student? Can you teach me the Bow and Arrow?" And the woman replied, "I accepted you as my student the very first day you peeked through the window." Thus, Hidayah trained with the Master Archer for several years. She was on the path to becoming a very strong, yet gentle, archer.

## 1

# The Preparation

It was the middle of July. The Jannah Jewels, on summer break from school, were gathered around the kitchen table at Jaide's house.  In front of them, spread out on the table, was an old-looking map. Iman had the *Book of Knowledge* in front of her, and looked back and forth between it and the map. She was looking up each of the names on the map, getting ready to face the challenges ahead by arming herself with background knowledge of the place they would be going to. Jaide was completing a sketch of the artifact they were supposed to find on this adventure, having copied it from the map. Sara meditated silently, drawing together her inner courage for what lay ahead. And Hidayah?  Hidayah seemed to be focused on her compass. In her eyes there was a look of determination. But her body

language told another story – her hands played nervously with the compass, turning it over and over.

"Ready to go to on our next adventure, Jewels?" asked Iman breaking the silence.

Sara and Hidayah drew deep breaths.

"Sure," Jaide answered confidently, slurping up her strawberry banana smoothie. "I'm always up for a challenge." She gave her friends a charming smile.

Jaide was half-serious and half-joking. The last adventure in Baghdad had been a difficult one for her; she had been tested with her most valuable possession: her artist pen. Amazingly, Jaide had been able to give it up in the end, allowing the Jannah Jewels to complete their mission successfully. And then, Jaide had been rewarded by getting something even better than what she had given up.

*That was the lesson in it all,* thought Jaide. *If you give something up that you love, for the greater good, God will replace it for you with something that is better!* She smiled warmly at the memory of it all. The best part had to be receiving her new pen from the Master Artist. What an honour!

Hidayah stood up.

"Iman, the *Book of Knowledge*?" she asked.

"Check!" said Iman.

"And the time travel watch, Jaide?" asked Hidayah.

"Check!" said Jaide.

"And that mysterious metal ball of yours, Sara?" asked Hidayah.

"Check! Check!" said Sara.

"What about you? Are you just going to stare at that compass or bring it along?" asked Iman.

"Check!" smiled Hidayah. "I am bringing it of course."

Hidayah carefully took her bamboo container from around her neck. Iman helped her roll up the ancient map and place it in the container, which Hidayah put back round her neck. Finally, Hidayah slung her bow and arrow over her shoulder. Her dark eyebrows furrowed the way they did when she was serious.

Jaide put her sketchbook and her new artist pen into her backpack. Sara refilled her water canteen and put on some lip balm to protect her lips from chapping. Iman pushed her eyeglasses back onto her nose and put the *Book of Knowledge* into her backpack.

"Let's go Jannah Jewels!" said Hidayah, heading toward the front door.

Just then Jaide's mother, Mrs. Yin, walked into the kitchen.

"Asalaamu alaykum. It's a lovely sunny day today, why the long faces?" she asked.

"Walaikum asalaam Mrs. Yin," said the girls in unison.

"Long faces? No long faces here," said Sara, putting an extra cheeriness into her voice. The girls made an effort to smile and act casual.

"What are you up to today, Sweethearts?" asked Mrs. Yin curiously.

"Oh, we're just going to ancient Spain, to play our role in ensuring peace in the world! We need to pick up an important artifact on the way, and we have to do it before time runs out or you might never see us again! But, don't worry we should be back before you know it," said Iman.

The Jannah Jewels glared at Iman and then looked up at Mrs. Yin, waiting for her reaction.

Mrs. Yin examined the faces of the Jannah Jewels. "You girls sure do have a great imagination…" said Mrs. Yin, but she did not sound sure of her own words. Fortunately for the Jannah Jewels, the doorbell rang at that moment. It was Jaide's little sister who had come home from Art class. Greeting her little sister with a high five and hug, Jaide seized the moment.

"Okay Mom, see you later *inshaAllah!* Can't wait to have your hotpot tonight! Asalaamu alaykum!" Jaide gave her Mom a hug.

The Jannah Jewels all gave the parting salutation of "peace be upon you" to Mrs. Yin. The girls hadn't always been so proper about their interactions with adults, but since becoming the Jannah Jewels, Sensei had taught them that respect for elders – including Parents, Teachers, Grandparents - was a key to success. *When you serve the elders, you receive blessings in your life. When you honor those who have more wisdom than you, you are granted the wisdom to see, and do, right. And your life becomes easier.*

The girls knew they needed as much of *that* kind of blessing as they could get, especially when they were about to embark on a new mission – a mission that seemed, from all they had heard about it, much harder than any other in the past.

The Jannah Jewels sprinted from Jaide's house to the neighbourhood park. The sun was just dipping past its peak, which meant it was just after noon. Sparrows glided across the sky, racing, dancing, diving and soaring. Young children played on the swings nearby. In the distance they could hear the melody of the ice-cream truck slowly approaching.

"Let's get back in time for the ice-cream truck!" said Jaide.

Hidayah gave Jaide a tough look.

"Or at least…for dinner. I think my Mom's cooking hotpot tonight!" Jaide was not stubborn – Hidayah loved how flexible she could be, and how it showed through even in her jokes and comments – in big things and in small.

"I wonder what it will be like in Ancient Spain," mused Sara.

"Well," said Iman. "It was a place where Muslims, Jews and Christians lived and learned together peacefully for a long time."

"Just like in Baghdad!" said Sara.

"Wait til you see the libraries of Andalusia!" said Iman.

"Andalusia?" said Sara.

"Oh, Andalusia is another name for Ancient Spain," said Iman. "It comes from the Arabic name Al-Andalus."

"It's so amazing how different a place is when we get there – how, no matter how much we read about it before arriving, it's always much more than what we could have imagined once we actually get there."

"Yeah," said Jaide. "I guess it goes to show you: never judge a time period by what the history books say! Ha ha!"

"Alright girls, the ice cream truck is getting closer! There's no time to lose! Let's move!" Hidayah threw a smile at Jaide and started to run towards a maple tree in the distance.

The Jannah Jewels ran past babies on swings, mothers with their strollers and children playing soccer. They carefully slipped between the long branches of the maple tree and pushed against the bark of the trunk with all their might.

Down, down, down they slid until they bumped and all fell over into an underground cave.

"They have got to find a better way to time travel," said Jaide rubbing her back.

"Asalamu alaykum!" said a familiar voice.

They looked behind them. It was the Master Archer dressed in her long red flowing robes. She looked radiant as always.

"Walaikum asalaam!" said the Jannah Jewels.

"Are you ready for your next adventure – this time to Andalusia?" she asked.

The Master Archer held up an old piece of paper. It was falling apart. There, in the center of the page, was a picture of a bottle with an ornate stopper. There was some kind of powder inside.

"You must find the artifact before Jaffar does – this you know. But girls, you will face some surprises on this mission, and you will be challenged in ways you have never been before," Sensei paused. "You will keep receiving messages that will guide you along the way. Listen well for them."

The Master Archer looked at Hidayah with mercy in her eyes, "I want you to remember: Always ask of God. Whatever you are doing, ask for His Assistance. And when you ask God, ask with your whole heart, and then have no fear. Trust that He will help you."

Hidayah's eyes were fixed on Sensei, as she tried to drink in each word, to absorb the light that seemed to be coming from Sensei's face.

"Go," Sensei said gently. "You must rush. If you don't make it back in time, you could be stuck there forever. Go!"

*Why did the last warning from Sensei seem so eerie this time*? Hidayah wondered.

Hidayah stood up and said bravely, "Jannah Jewels, let's go!"

The Jannah Jewels joined hands in a circle.

"Are you alright, Hidayah?" Iman whispered. "Your palms are sweating and so hot."

"Yes, I'm fine. Let's get going already!" Hidayah whispered back.

*"Bismillah-irRahman-irRahim!"*

**2**

# Landing

The Jannah Jewels opened their eyes. They were lying down on their backs, above them the star-strewn heavens, so clear that they could even see planets. Suddenly a fork of lightening flashed across the sky, and a loud clap of thunder followed. The girls sprung to their feet and started to instinctively run for the nearest shelter but when they got close, they realized they were face to face with a giant... bookshelf!

"What's going on?" screamed Iman.

"Asalaamu alaykum," said a voice coming towards them. "There's nothing to be afraid of."

Suddenly the black sky disappeared and light

surrounded them. The girls were stunned.

*Have I died*? wondered Hidayah.

A man was now standing before them. He was wearing a long white tunic and a turban. His face was wrinkled and wise. He smiled.

"My name is Abbas ibn Firnas. You must be the Jannah Jewels. Welcome."

"What is this place?" asked Hidayah looking around. Her eyes were now adjusting and she could see the giant bookshelf, and around it some simple furniture. She realized they were inside a room.

"It is my home – welcome! It is also a planetarium of sorts – something I set up so that people could come and learn about the celestial bodies in a more close-up way. The stars and planets, the thunder and lightning, these are all simulations created by tools I have in my basement."

"What?" cried out Jaide. "How is that even possible? A planetarium?! This is the 9th century!"

Abbas smiled. "It is all only possible if God wills it, and by His Permission. I am blessed to have been given Permission to do all this."

Abbas gestured towards an open door, "But come now, please, before we talk further, have a seat in the garden and take some refreshment."

The girls followed Abbas through the door and down a hallway leading to a courtyard. As they walked, Iman whispered to Jaide, "You think *that* was impossible – just wait til you get this: he's the first man to fly!"

**3**

## Unravelling the Secrets

Out in the sunshine of the courtyard, to Jaide's delight, the girls were served a colourful and delicious meal of rice and fish. Iman whispered, "I think this is paella – a dish still popular in Spain to this day!"

Jaide was too busy enjoying the meal to say much. Sara was looking all around, awed by the many species of trees surrounding them in the courtyard. Hidayah was thinking of Sensei's parting words of advice.

The Jannah Jewels' host looked lost in thought. After his warm welcome, he seemed to go into his own world. Suddenly, a dove flew into the courtyard. Abbas ibn Firnas looked up, watching as it fluttered

in the air.  He smiled a broad smile.  Then he spoke.

"For more than twenty years, I have been watching the way that objects, such as this bird, move through the air. I've observed seeds, leaves, feathers, bats and birds. And I have tried to become one of them."

The girls looked at each other, and then back at Abbas.

"What I mean is: I have been building a flying machine, for the past twenty years. And, with God's Permission, I am ready now. Tomorrow, *inshaAllah*, I will go to the Sierra Morena and attempt flight, by the Permission of the Most High!"

"Fly?!" asked Jaide, her fork held mid-air.

Abbas smiled at her, "Many people think something is impossible, until it is tried and shown to be possible.  I believe flying is possible, even for us humans."

Jaide muttered: "Well yes, one day that will be the way *most* people get from Vancouver to Cordoba, but…"

Iman piped up, "The Sierra Morena, where is that, Sir?"

"It's a range of hills just outside Cordoba. It's also called Jebal al Arous. You know, I tried flying once, twenty years ago. And since then, I have not made such a public attempt. But this time, God willing, many people of Cordoba will be coming to see how my flight goes."

Abbas turned suddenly to the Jannah Jewels.

"Will you pray for me?"

"Yes!"

"Of course!"

"Absolutely"

Definitely, Sir!"

Abbas smiled at each one of them. There was a look of wistfulness in his eyes. He got up from the table, saying he would go inside and bring back some tea and dessert. Iman took the opportunity to pull out the *Book of Knowledge*. She opened it and quickly scanned the page before her.

"*Abbas ibn Firnas was the first person in history*

*to fly with a machine.*"

"Wow," muttered Jaide. "You mean he beat the Wright Brothers to it?"

"Sure did - only by about 1050 years," Iman smiled. Then her smile suddenly faded. She looked up at the girls. "There are different accounts of what happened. All of them say he succeeded in making the first flight ever…but some accounts say he took off from a wall at the Sierra Morena, and was able to land back on it safely. And…and…some accounts say that he got very badly injured…because he tried to land on the ground but did not slow down enough before landing."

"Oh no!" said Jaide.

Hidayah turned to her and said quietly: "Jaide, everything that happens to us in life is God's destiny for us."

"But," said Jaide, "we can always pray, and by our prayers, God brings us a better outcome than if we hadn't prayed."

"Let's pray that Abbas doesn't get hurt," said Sara.

Jaide added, "Yes, I like the wall version of this story. There's no reason why *it* isn't the true history. Let's pray for it."

Abbas came back into the courtyard with a tray of steaming mint tea and bowls of nuts and candied pumpkin.

"I feel like I'm in Jannah," said Jaide with a happy smile on her face.

"Well, we *are* the Jannah Jewels," said Sara, with a giggle.

"Jannah Jewels! Forgive me my daughters, I have been a terrible host. What is it I can help you with? You seem worried and I know you also have your own mission to complete. Tell me about it." said Abbas.

"Well, Sir, we are looking for a bottle of…" started out Iman, but she was at a loss for how to describe the artifact correctly. Jaide pulled out her sketch of it, and showed it to Abbas.

"Hmm. A vial of…something. A vial of what?" he looked inquiringly at the girls.

No one answered.

"There's definitely something inside this vial. Do you have *any* idea what it is?" Abbas asked gently.

Now as they looked at the drawing, it dawned on the Jannah Jewels that unlike other artifacts of past journeys, this one had two important components – both the inner and the outer.

The bottle itself was plain glass with a stopper on top. The stopper was a beautifully-carved rounded knob. Inside, there was a powder-like material. That substance was at least as important as the bottle that carried it!

"We don't know, Sir," Hidayah answered finally, pulling the map out of its bamboo case, and spreading it out before Abbas.

"Hmmmm," said Abbas. "I see. The picture on this map is too faded to tell what the substance is. The colour doesn't show."

"How will we ever know what to search for?" exclaimed Sara in a worried tone. "There could be millions of little bottles like this, all over this place. Just like last time there were so many pens - but only *one* right one."

"My daughters, look closely. What do you see?"

The girls were silent.

"Observe. What can you tell me about this bottle?"

"Umm…it's see-through," said Jaide.

"It has a fancy lid," said Sara.

"Yes! That's it. The lid tells you its identity. You see, the pharmacists, perfume sellers, spice merchants, and general supply shopkeepers of Andalusia all sell their products in bottles, and they use the bottle stoppers like a label or trademark so the buyer remembers who he bought the bottle from. Each seller or supplier has his own style. Some bottle tops are very plain, some are engraved with initials, some are shaped like flowers or mosaic designs, some are inlaid with gold and silver, and *some*-" Abbas paused and smiled, "-are carved like this one.

"If my eyes don't deceive me," Abbas peered closely at the image on the map. "This one is from the store of an old and dear friend of mine!"

"Oh wonderful!" said Sarah. The Jannah Jewels looked visibly relieved.

"Yes," said Abbas. "This bottle comes from the store of my friend Yeshua ben Yosef. He sells a wide range of bottled products, all with this signature lid of his."

"So…does that mean…everyone knows that this kind of lid means Yeshua's store?" Hidayah was thinking of Jaffar. Would Jaffar be able to ask someone and find out right away that the bottle was from Yeshua, just like they had?

"Some brands, my daughter, are more famous than others. Yeshua is well-known to local inventors and scientists, because of the superior grade of his products. But most average Andalusians are not looking for scientific-grade products. They are happy with a middle-range product. So Yeshua remains a bit of a hidden gem."

"We know the origin of the bottle now, but have no idea what material is inside. How will we ever know which of the many bottles in Yeshua's store is the right one?" asked Iman.

"Well my daughter, let us approach your question with a scientific mind. We will present several options and then, by a process of elimination, determine which is the most probable to be the substance in the bottle. Will you join me?"

The Jannah Jewels nodded. Jaide whispered to Sara, "I think this is an ancient form of brainstorming."

Sara whispered back, "Actually, I think it is a step in the scientific method."

"We begin by allowing our minds to be freed for a moment. We let any thoughts that come to us from God, His Inspiration to us, to flow into our brains. So close your eyes, and let the doors of your minds open. *Bismillah*. What could this substance be?"

Jaide, Iman, Hidayah and Sara closed their eyes and allowed their minds to relax. Hidayah felt so peaceful. She realized she had been feeling pressure to rush through this journey and reach its conclusion. Now she let herself be calm. Their eyes closed, the girls let their minds be filled with possibilities. They spoke as each idea came.

"Sand."

"Sulphur."

"Henna."

"Salt."

"Sugar."

"Icing sugar…mmm."

"Cumin."

"Dust."

"Turmeric."

"Pepper."

"Baking soda."

"Gold dust."

"Silver shavings."

"Ambergris"

"Sawdust."

"Gunpowder."

"Cinnamon...mmm."

"Ground cloves."

"Crimson."

"Talcum."

As they became quiet again, Abbas said, "*Alhamdulillah.*" After a pause, he continued, "In order to now determine which matter would most probably be in the bottle, I need to ask you, what kinds of artifacts do you usually need to bring back from the places you visit?"

Hidayah thought. "I think they are always things that are special to the place we visit."

Iman piped up, "Or the *time in history* that we visit."

Sara finished, "Or the *people* who live in that time and place."

Abbas's face crinkled with a smile. "I understand. You have three criteria to choose from: the artifact must have a connection to a) the place, b) the time, or c) the people you visit on that mission. So, out of all the substances you named while we had our eyes closed, which one do you think is special to the time, place or people here in Andalusia?"

No one spoke. Then Iman spoke in a high and excited voice. "Ambergris or crimson! They are the two substances that are very unique to Andalusia and this era. They are highly valued. The ambergris available in Cordoba is famous! And so is the crimson."

"What are they, anyway?" asked Jaide. "I thought crimson was a color!"

"It is," said Iman, opening up the Book of Knowledge. "It says here that crimson, called Qirmiz, was a famous product of Al Andalus. *It was made of the dried bodies of the Kermes insect, which were gathered commercially in Mediterranean countries. The insects live on the Kermes oak. They feed on its sap and the females produce a red dye that is the source of natural crimson. Crimson was sold throughout Europe, in granular form, and was used to provide a beautiful rich red to textiles. It was highly prized, and the best quality Qirmiz – at the best price – was available in Cordoba. Merchants from all over Europe would come here to buy this color to transform their cloths, leathers, and wools to beautiful reds and oranges. Carmine, made of the cochineal insect, eventually overtook crimson in popularity, coming into Europe in 1549.*"

"And ambergris?"

"It's a waxy substance produced by the sperm whale that washes up on beaches and is collected by people. It is often turned into a powder. *A prized material used for medicinal purposes, it was considered to provide a cure for many ailments. Additionally, it would prolong the fragrance of a perfume, so it was often added to perfumes.* It was collected along the Mediterranean coast, on the beaches, and supplied to the rest of the world from here!"

"What colour is it?" asked Jaide.

"Grey," answered Abbas ibn Firnas.

The girls were silent.

Iman added: "It's got to be one of these... special substances. These Andalusian specialties. I just don't think we'd be sent all the way here to find a bottle of... well, sand or salt! You know?"

"Unless, said Abbas, speaking very slowly. "Unless that salt *was special* – it may not be special to the time and place, but what if it were special to the persons you are visiting? In that case, it would meet

32

one of your three conditions for being an artifact...."

Hidayah thought for a moment, and then said, "Do *you* like salt, sir?"

Abbas laughed warmly. "Oh no, not especially, my little daughter! But think closely about the other things you mentioned. For example, you said henna. Now, if you had been visiting my sister, instead of me, your bottle could very well contain henna – a product commonly used by women of Andalusia. Think about all the possibilities; don't jump too quickly to conclusions."

"Huh? I don't get it," said Jaide.

"Well, my sister uses henna for her hair and to dye her hands on special occasions like weddings, Eid, and other celebrations. This means that henna has a connection to her. You see, a material may at first have no importance to us, but when it is connected with a person who is in some way important to us, it becomes special! "

"Just like the pen – our artifact in Baghdad! It wasn't special to Baghdad or that historical era – it was special because of who it belonged to!"

"And your pen, Jaide, was special to you because it was *yours.* And you found it hard to give away."

"And I love my new pen because *someone special* gave it to me"

Hidayah smiled. It was true. The objects that were important to her were important because of who they were connected to.

Iman spoke up, "Tell us more about ambergris. It seems to be the most likely option, Sir."

"Well, if you insist. I will offer you this: ambergris could very well be the most unique substance to this location and time; and I can attest that it is highly sought-after and very expensive. Ambergris has medicinal uses and is also burned to make sweet smells, distributed by kings, sent to loved ones as a gift, and prolongs musk and perfumes – so it certainly is used for a wide range of purposes and almost all households in Andalusia have used it at some time. Crimson is also valuable and a product of our own land here, and we are world-famous for it; but its use is limited to craftspeople."

Iman said excitedly, "It sounds exactly like what

an artifact should be!"

"Before we can conclude that, is there anything else you could tell me that would help to support or put doubt to our hypothesis?"

There was something else that was on Hidayah's mind. *Maybe Jaffar knows...he too is looking... maybe this time he knows more than we do about the artifact.*

"Sir, there's something I need to mention. There is someone else who is looking for the same artifact. And he...he might know more than we do," said Hidayah.

"Is there any way you can meet this person and find out whether he knows what's inside the bottle?"

Jaide started to answer, "Oh Jaffar is a real—" but Hidayah cut her off. "We can try. Perhaps if we go out into town today, we might catch sight of him and go from there."

Abbas ibn Firnas smiled. "That is exactly what I was about to suggest - that you go into town today, as I would like to send you to Yeshua ben Yosef. As it happens, one of Yeshua's most sought-after products is ambergris. He carries the best in town! He also carries crimson. If you find out from Jaffar what he knows about the substance inside the vial – any information – the colour even -" Abbas scanned the girls' faces and read their feelings. "Well, should it be difficult to *ask* this Jaffar, then *observe*, my daughters, just observe and let yourselves be guided by the signs the Most High sends you."

# 4

## In Town

The girls made their way from the lovely home of Abbas ibn Firnas into the main part of the city. The clean avenues were lined with trees. In their generous shade were clusters of stores, medical and dental offices, artisanal workshops, and small restaurants. Horses and mules pulling carts or carrying loads in burlap bags clip-clopped along the cobbled streets. Sara was enthralled by the beauty of each horse and mule; she couldn't help but feel that life was better when horses ruled the roads, not cars.

Abbas ibn Firnas had said that Yeshua's store was in the large square plaza at the entrance to the marketplace. Before long, the Jannah Jewels found themselves inside the busy market. It seemed they

had entered from the exit, and would not have to go all the way through it in order to reach the entrance on the other side.

In the bustle of the market, the girls' senses were flooded with new sounds and smells and sights. On both sides of the narrow market lane were craft workshops and stalls. In some of the workshops, men hammered away at metal, fashioning from it shields and swords as well as tables, teapots, and ornaments. Silversmiths tinkered, turning silver into jewelry.

Soon the girls entered an area of the market dedicated to medicine. These stalls were filled with big sacks of herbs and leaves. Further down, Hidayah could see stalls lined with rows of bottles containing all sorts of powders and liquids. Suddenly Hidayah heard a voice that made her blood go cold.

"I'm looking for this! THIS and nothing else. I want a bottle that looks EXACTLY like this one!" It was Jaffar, about ten feet away from the Jannah Jewels. He was standing in front of the stalls that sold the bottles. Three shopkeepers had come out from behind their counters, to look at the map Jaffar was holding. Jaffar pointed at the image on the map. The shopkeepers shook their heads.

"I'm sorry, we don't have a bottle that looks like this. You are welcome to buy what we do have, though."

Another shopkeeper said, "Maybe you need to try the perfume market, they might have fancy bottles like this."

The third one added, "Or the women's cosmetics market – it could be a bottle of henna."

When Jaffar heard the words 'women's cosmetics,' he started to fume. "What do you think I am doing, shopping for Mother's day? This is really important. This bottle is, is - *a treasure*!"

Hidayah somehow felt his words bolstered their hypothesis about the ambergris. If anything was a treasure, it was this rare substance.

Jaffar was struggling to control his anger. He lowered his voice and said something that Hidayah was too far away to catch. She quickly motioned to the Jannah Jewels to enter the surrounding stores and hide, while she advanced forward, concealed in the crowds, until she was just close enough to hear Jaffar.

"I plead with you, sirs. Just give me your best guess. What does it look like to you? You have the expert pharmacists' eyes. What is in the bottle?" and he pointed once more to the image on the map.

The shopkeepers peered closer at the paper, trying to discern what was shown on it.

They had no idea. "We are sorry, sir, we cannot tell you. You must *know* that which you seek, *before* you come and seek it."

*He doesn't know what the powder is! We're ahead of him!* Hidayah thought, grateful that they had landed in Abbas's hands, and that he had helped them solve at least part of the mystery of the artifact.

Hidayah entered a store just opposite where Jaffar was standing and pretended to be a customer examining the wares. Out of the corner of her eye, she saw Moe and Slim catch up to Jaffar. Jaffar was now done his questioning of the shopkeepers, but ordered Moe and Slim to do one last search of all the bottles in the three stores – paying close attention to the lids.

Jaffar himself moved on, and Hidayah saw him walk past the store she was in, grumbling and frustrated.

When Hidayah was sure the coast was clear and Jaffar and his goons had moved far away into the marketplace, going in the opposite direction to theirs, Hidayah went back for her friends. They gathered once more and made their way with a quick pace towards the entrance of the market.  Iman asked Hidayah what had happened. All Hidayah could say was, "We know this, Jaffar doesn't know what's in the bottle – and he has no idea which store the bottle is from."

Finally the Jannah Jewels reached the arch that was the marketplace entrance. They were in a wide square, with shops on each side. They split up into twos, each pair taking on two sides of the square. Very quickly, Hidayah and Iman covered their half of the square, not finding Yeshua's store.

Sara and Jaide were much slower, because Jaide

was hungry! Every time they passed by a sweet-stall, Jaide pointed at the various types of pastries, cookies and candies on display. Each shopkeeper obliged her interest, providing her a taste of what she pointed at, until she had tried more varieties than Sara could keep count of.

Sara tried to tug Jaide past another stall. "Enough already, Jaide! You're going to make yourself ill."

Jaide could only say, licking her sticky fingers, "These are the BEST sweets I have ever tasted. Andalusia, you are amaaaazing! I think I could live here."

Hidayah and Iman, rounding their third side of the square, soon met up with Jaide and Sara. As they stood together in a group, they looked up to see where they had reached - and there above them was a sign that said: *Yeshua's Supplies. Alhamdulilah!* Hidayah made a quick prayer that they'd find what they had come in search of.

It was dark inside the store, but soon the girls' eyes adjusted. There were shelves upon shelves lining the walls, from the floor to the ceiling. The shelves were crowded with lines of bottles in all different sizes - some stout and some tall, some tiny and some large. Bunches of dried herbs hung from the rafters, and cloth bags full of leaves and flower petals crowded the floor. There was a musty medicinal smell in the air.

A small man emerged from a back room, and said: "Salam, Shalom, welcome!"

The girls replied politely, and Hidayah spoke up, "We are looking for Mr. Yeshua."

"Indeed, that is me."

"Sir, we are friends of Abbas ibn Firnas; he sent us to you for a bottle of – er, ambergris that we are looking for."

"Oh ho!" said Yeshua with a joyful laugh. "My dear friend Abbas wants only the best, is it so?" And he turned around, examining the bottles on the shelves behind him.

"Ambergris…do you know how great and special is ambergris? I will tell you. But wait. First, have a seat." And he brought out four stools from behind the counter.

The girls sat down, though Hidayah was starting to worry about the time. The shadows were getting longer. In her nervousness, halfway through Yeshua's account of the qualities and uses of ambergris, Hidayah turned round to check the sun's height in the sky. As she turned, she caught sight of a pair of watching eyes, peering in from outside the store.

The eyes were a stinging steel grey, and seemed like they held many secrets.

*I know these eyes,* thought Hidayah.

In a flash, the eyes moved. The watcher had changed locations, but Hidayah was sure he or she was still there, and listening. Hidayah wondered if it was Moe or Slim.

"...and that is why ambergris is such a valuable and beneficial substance, girls," Yeshua concluded. He laughed a jolly laugh again. "Now, can I offer you some to purchase?"

At the same moment as Hidayah stood up to check who and where the watcher was, Yeshua brought out a bottle that looked exactly like the one shown on the map.

Before Hidayah could warn her that they were being spied on, Jaide cried out loudly, "That's the one!"

Hidayah gripped her arm to quiet her. "What, Hidayah?" said Jaide, annoyed.

Before anything else could happen, a stranger walked into the store. She was wearing a satin grey dress, the same color as...her eyes! It was the spy! She had walked into plain view!

The girl in the satin dress looked briefly at the Jannah Jewels, and then spoke directly to Yeshua: "Good afternoon, Sir. I want to buy that bottle of ambergris. I need it."

"Oh ho," said Yeshua with a jolly smile. "It looks like I have several customers who want the same product. It is a rare product, and my stocks are a bit low. In fact, I only have this one bottle left. Madame in the grey dress, I am sorry, but these customers were here before you."

"I need it!" cried the girl and she reached for it, knocking down two other bottles that were standing on the counter.

"Oh ho, just a minute," said Yeshua lifting the little bottle out of reach.

Jaide stood up. "No way are you having it. *We* need it and we were here first."

The girl with the grey eyes looked down. "Sir, forgive me, forgive my action just now…but you don't understand!" Her voice started to rise and tremble at the same time. "It's my Father – I fear what will happen if I can't bring this to him."

Yeshua looked concerned. "Ah. Your father is sick? Perhaps you should tell me the symptoms. I could suggest another medicine that could be of help…."

"No, it's only this…ambergris. This is the one I need."

Yeshua looked at the Jannah Jewels, his eyes searching theirs.

No one spoke, and the tension hung thick in the air.

Hidayah stood up. "Perhaps we could split it. You could have some and we -"

Before she could finish, the girl cut her off in a harsh tone, "No way! I need it all!" and again, she tried to grab the bottle from Yeshua's hand.

Yeshua held it away from her.

"Well," said Yeshua. "Frankly, we have a conflict here. Let us ask my neighbor shopkeeper, both a friend and a wise elder, what to do."

Yeshua walked out from behind the counter and out of the store, bottle in hand. The Jannah Jewels and the girl in the grey dress followed behind Yeshua. To Hidayah's amazement, the store that Yeshua had led them into was an archery supply store. Bows and arrows of all sizes and shapes hung from the ceiling and stood propped against walls.

Two gasps came in a row: first, Hidayah's and then...another.

The old man at the back of the shop came forward to greet Yeshua. Yeshua quickly explained the problem.

The old man looked first at Hidayah and then at the girl in the grey dress. He smiled and said, "I see you are both practitioners of the bow and arrow."

Indeed, Hidayah now saw that the girl in the grey dress was carrying on her back a small bow and arrow.

The old man continued, "I suggest you untie this knot you are in with the clear string of a bow and the pure end of an arrow."

He looked at Yeshua and said, "Put an empty bottle on a fencepost, and have each of the two contestants stand at a fair distance. Whoever can strike the bottle with the arrow is the winner and can have what they seek."

Yeshua turned to the Jannah Jewels and the girl in the grey dress. "Does this suit you?" he asked. "Not quite a duel, but a fair contest."

Before Hidayah could say anything, the girl in the grey dress spoke, "I agree!" She flashed her eyes confidently at Hidayah.

Hidayah had no choice.

"I agree as well."

**5**

## The Test

There was a loud crash as the bottle came down in smithereens. The girl in the grey dress turned and smiled at Hidayah. The Jannah Jewels looked at each other nervously, and then smiled encouragingly at Hidayah. *This girl has a good shot,* thought Hidayah.

Yeshua placed another empty bottle on the same post, and Hidayah came into position. She remembered the words of her Master: *Aim with your heart....*

Swoosh! The arrow went flying through the air. It hit the bottle at its base. The bottle toppled, still intact, off the post. As it hit the ground, it finally broke.

Hidayah looked at Yeshua. Yeshua smiled. "Well, I think you are both equal in this."

The girl in the grey dress flashed her eyes. "No, we are not. I broke the bottle on impact - I was able to hit it full-on. Hidayah did not."

"Hey, how do you know my name?" asked Hidayah.

But before she could get an answer, the girl in the grey dress turned and fled. Without being able to put it into words, Hidayah knew what was about to happen. When Yeshua had gone back to the store to get the empty bottles for the contest, he must have left the ambergris back in the store. The girl in the grey dress was now running - running back towards the store.

"Hey, come back here," called out Jaide.

The Jannah Jewels started running after the girl. But by the time they reached the store, the girl was gone, and so was the bottle.

## 6

## The Baker's Cart

The Jannah Jewels, feeling dejected and lost, walked aimlessly down the streets of Cordoba.

"We're doomed," said Jaide. "We've lost the artifact. That girl probably lives in some home or palace in these parts and we will have no way of even seeing her again. The houses here don't even have big windows you can see into. They are just plain walls with super high windows that are covered from the outside. We'll never even be able to spy her out."

"There's a wisdom in that kind of privacy, Jaide," said Iman. "Inside the high walls are whole other worlds, like the garden at Abbas's house; and the high walls keep out the heat of the summer and the cold of the winter."

"Okay, but, right now, they spell doom for us." said Jaide. Hidayah's heart sank. Maybe it was all her fault. She hadn't hit her target properly.

"Doom?! No, we can't be all doom and gloom. Not this soon! Weren't you the one, Jaide, who said that prayer makes a difference?" Sara reminded her.

"Yes, let's pray," said Jaide. "All is not lost."

Iman joined in, "God will make a way for us. Trust Him. And expect the best from Him!"

Hidayah suddenly recalled the words of her Sensei about the art of great expectations. It had been a rainy Vancouver morning, Hidayah remembered, and she had been worried about a test she had that day at school. Sensei had said, *You must always expect the best from God. If you expect goodness from Him in every moment, you will not be disappointed. In any situation, always have trust that He will give you the outcome you hope for.*

*And if He doesn't?* Hidayah had asked.

*If He doesn't give you that which you hoped for,*

*know that He is giving you that which is* better *for you. Because He knows what is best for you, and He loves you.*

Hidayah felt the hope come back to her. She tried to let go of the one thought that was still bothering her: how did the grey-dressed girl know her name?

Just as Hidayah's nerves were slowly calming down, Iman gave a cry, "Oh no!"

Up ahead, the crowds in the street seemed to part. Three fast moving thugs, whom the Jannah Jewels knew only too well, were walking towards them, their eyes clearly set on their targets.

"Oh God," breathed Hidayah.

"Come on, let's get out of here," said Jaide.

The Jannah Jewels scrambled. They turned this way and that, weaving through winding streets, but they could hear Jaffar, Moe and Slim close behind them, calling out their names.

The Jannah Jewels at last turned a corner and found the perfect place to hide. It was a large cart hitched to the back of a mule, parked outside a bakery. The girls swifty climbed onto the cart and hid themselves under a heavy oilcloth.  There were fresh loaves, buns, and flatbread all around them.

"Perfect cart to hide in," said Jaide licking her lips.

"These need to be taken back to the Art School right away," they heard the baker instruct the two men at the front of the cart.  "Don't be late."

"Perfect!" whispered Jaide. "We just got our own ride to an art school! This is a dream come true! I love this mission!"

"I thought you wanted to be home for your Mom's hotpot!" exclaimed Iman. Jaide was too busy reaching out to grab a large piece of bread to answer. Sara swatted Jaide's hand in an attempt to stop her.

The cart suddenly jerked forward and the girls had to hold onto each other to not roll over into the loaves. Through the opening at the back of the cart, the Jannah Jewels saw that Jaffar, Moe and Slim had reached the bakery now and were questioning the baker. They saw the baker shrug his shoulders and shake his head.

Hidayah let relief wash over her: at a mule's pace, but surely, they were headed to safety. After about half an hour, the girls peeked out from under the cloth, and found that they had left the busy streets of the city and were now on a dirt road winding up a hill. Emerald fields rolled majestically in all directions. Sara whispered poetically about the beauty of the scene.

All of a sudden, the cart jolted to a halt.

One cart driver jumped down off his seat, and called out to the other driver, "The cart seems a lot heavier than usual. The mules are moving so slowly!"

The girls huddled behind the stacks of bread as the man came towards the back of the cart.

*Please, God, please don't let us get caught right now,* pleaded Hidayah.

The cart driver peered under the oilcloth. The afternoon light was too dim for him to see much of anything under the heavy cloth. As he patted the stacks of bread back into neat piles, he just missed hitting Jaide's elbow which was sticking out at a crazy angle. She stifled a yelp. The man frowned and lowered the cloth, giving up on finding anything out of the ordinary.

"Hey, let's go Taufiq, we have to go deliver these before it's too late. The mules are just tired from the last trip," called out the second driver.

"Alright, alright - let's go," agreed Taufiq.

The girls breathed a deep sigh of relief. "Thank You God!" said Hidayah, relaxing her shoulders.

Sara reached out and grabbed Jaide's hand for what seemed to Jaide like the hundredth time that day. "What now?" asked Jaide. "I just want a little -" But Sara was looking at the time-travel watch on Jaide's wrist.

"We need to get back to the tree real soon," said Sara. "There are only two hours left. Maybe we'll have to leave without the artifact."

Jaide said, "This is by far the craziest adventure! But it's also the best!"

Iman was looking at Hidayah, whose face was a mask of worry. "*InshaAllah,*" whispered Iman. "*InshaAllah*, it will all work out. Don't give up!"

CRAAAAASH! BANG! BOING!

"Woah!"

"Ooof!"

The cart had hit some stones on the dirt road, and the girls were thrown about amongst the stacks of bread. As the cart ground to a standstill, they could hear the voices of the drivers, coaxing and urging the mules to continue up the road. But the mules would not budge.

"I told you pulling this cart was too much for them," said Taufiq.

"Aw, they are just being stubborn – keep them going, we are almost there!"

"No, I think we should pause and give them some water and a rest. It's not right to treat animals like this!"

"Oh fine, but not for more than five minutes, alright? The Art School students will be waiting for their evening meal!"

The girls peeked out from under their cover. They were dazzled by the landscape that was now turned golden by the close-to-sunset rays.

"*SubhanAllah*," whispered Sara.

And then, without any warning sign, someone's hand was grabbing Sara and lifting her out of the cart!

"We meet again Jannah Jewels," growled Slim quietly, holding Sara in his grip.

Moe flashed his teeth in a silent smile as he grabbed Hidayah with one hand and Iman with the other. Jaffar leapt out of the shadows and before Jaide could move, he had her trapped.

With all four girls out of the cart, it suddenly jolted forward, the mules able to pull it easily. Taufiq and the other driver said at the same time: "*Alhamdulillah.*"

**7**

## Identity Revealed

Jaffar, Slim and Moe had carted their hostages, hands clamped over their mouths, quickly away from the dirt path, so no one – including Taufiq and his partner – would be able to hear them if they tried to scream. Now they set them down. Jaffar spoke, "You know what we want girls. Hand over the artifact, and you can go free."

"Just let us go, Jaffar," responded Hidayah. She kept her voice low, and struggled hard to stay calm. Sensei had taught her a technique of staying calm and redirecting the energy used by her opponent against her.

"But we don't have it!" cried out Jaide.

"Don't play games with me. You know that in all our past missions, you've always discovered the artifact first. With only a few hours left in this mission, I find it hard to believe you don't have it safely in your possession. Now, if you want to ever make it back to your own world, you better give it to me without further delay."

"But we don't have it!" insisted Jaide. Sara nodded her head vigorously in support of Jaide's claim.

Suddenly, an arrow whizzed through the air, just missing Hidayah.

"Well, well, well," said a voice. And out of the darkness emerged the girl in the grey dress!

"My dear brother Jaffar," said the girl. "Did you just admit the Jannah Jewels usually outsmart you? Well, now, meet your true superior. And theirs! These girls aren't lying to you. They don't have the artifact! I do!"

"Jasmin!" said Jaffar. "What are you doing here? I can't believe this!"

"Jasmin?" said Sara.

61

*Now I know why those eyes looked so familiar,* thought Hidayah. *They match Jaffar's.*

Jasmin twirled around in her grey dress, her steel grey eyes piercing into Hidayah's.

*Hidayah. We're now officially introduced,* Jasmin's eyes seemed to say.

"So this is the person you can't seem to beat, eh Jaffar?" said Jasmin, motioning towards Hidayah. "Well, guess who beat her?"

But Jaffar had no ears for what Jasmin was saying. He was in shock.

"I can't believe Father didn't trust me and sent *you* through the time travel machine after me," said Jaffar.

"Hah! You can't be serious Jaffar! You've already failed three missions. It is time to end this battle once and for all," said Jasmin. "Just be lucky I came for you, to make sure you got out of this place and home safely. Come on, I've got the artifact, let's go."

"I won't let you be the one to take the artifact back to Father," said Jaffar.

"What? You have no choice, big brother."

"Jasmin, you don't know what you are doing. Give me the artifact!"

As Jaffar lunged towards Jasmin, she leapt away and took up a stance. Her bow and arrow were now drawn.

Jaffar took up a fighting stance too, and suddenly, Jasmin and Jaffar started shooting arrows at one another. Moe and Slim watched in disbelief. They tried to make Jaffar stop, but to no avail. The Jannah Jewels took their chance at the distraction. Jaide put down her skateboard and they quickly climbed on. Before Moe and Slim could grab them, the girls were speeding away.

Iman could sense Hidayah's tension. "Don't worry, Hidayah, trust in God. Remember the Sensei's words!"

## 8

## Shelter in the Great Mosque

Thoughts raced through Hidayah's mind.

*I wonder why Jasmin and Jaffar can't get along,* thought Hidayah. *You would think they would help each other since they are part of the same family.*

*Sensei would be so disappointed if I failed this mission. It was so important.*

*What would Abbas advise?*

Now at a safe distance far from their enemies, Jaide slowed down and gently brought the skateboard to a halt. They were in front of a huge building. They couldn't believe their eyes. It was the Great Mosque of Cordoba! They gazed up at its arches, held up by pillars made of red and white stone that resembled the rays of the sun. The prayer niche had glittering gold, blue and red mosaics.

Peace! The Jannah Jewels felt an ease wash over them as they entered the sanctuary and made their way to the fountains to wash for the sunset prayer. Their worries seemed to slip away with the water that rolled off their faces.

Inside the carpeted prayer space, they sat and listened to the Muezzin's call. Birds circled inside and outside the mosque, diving between arches and in the courtyard in the dimming light.

**9**

# Time is Running Out!

At the end of the prayer, Hidayah sat silently. She held her hands up, asking God with all her heart for the guidance they needed. *Oh Allah, please, please help us; the keys to all good are in Your Hands; anything hard can be made easy by You.* She felt certainty and hope fighting against the fear and worry inside her heart.

"I'm looking for someone," came a voice. "My sister. She has a bow and arrow. Could you tell her to come out and meet me here at the front entrance?"

Hidayah recognized the voice – it was Jaffar's. Now an old woman was coming purposefully towards Hidayah, and Hidayah realized that the old woman would think that she, Hidayah, was Jaffar's sister – since she was the only girl in the mosque with a bow and arrow on her back.

She jumped to her feet, and with her, the Jannah Jewels.

Her mind calm and clear, Hidayah instructed the Jewels, "Run! Through the courtyard!"

The Jewels took off, running through the courtyard and down a path to a grove of orange trees. They jumped over the low brick wall and ran between the gardens. Suddenly arrows filled the air around them. They had been detected and someone was shooting at them!

"Look!" cried Sara.

Up ahead of them was a small low building with a door in it. The Jannah Jewels ran for the door and leaned with all their might against it. With a groan it swung open, and the Jewels ducked inside. They bolted the door behind them.

Looking around, the girls found themselves at one end of a long hall lit with oil lamps.

"It's so quiet in here" said Iman, still trying to catch her breath. She slowly walked down the passageway. "*Bismillah!* There are steps here."

"Don't go any farther!" said Jaide. "Time is running out, we need to get out of here - and right now!"

"How do you know this isn't the way out?" said Iman anxiously.

Hidayah said calmly, "Girls, stay quiet and follow my lead. We can't go back now. We'll get caught by Jaffar. We need to go forward."

They started down the steep steps. The lamps lit their way as they descended. Finally, they reached the last step.

Even though oil lanterns glowed everywhere, it was hard to see at first. When their eyes got used to the strange light, their hearts nearly stopped.

"Oh!" gasped Iman.

They had come to a dead-end. They were trapped and now, from the end of the tunnel where they had entered, they could hear the sounds of someone banging at the bolted door, pounding it as if to break it down.

## 10

## The Secret Door

The Jannah Jewels stood frozen. What were they going to do? They had forgotten about the artifact and all they could think about was escaping Jaffar and getting back to the tree on time. If not, they would be stuck in Ancient Spain – forever!

"*Bismillah,*" said Hidayah – and she reached out to the wall in front of them. "Girls," she said, "It's not a dead end. There's another door here. It's just very old. I can feel the handle, but it seems to be locked."

"Quick, grab that lantern and shine it on the door," said Iman.

There were cobwebs, spiders, and dust covering the door. But it was beautifully carved old wood.

Hidayah felt the carvings with her hands.

"The door is locked, but where is the keyhole? How do we open it?" said Sara, holding the lantern close to the door.

Suddenly there was a faint crash from the other end of the tunnel, and the girls knew that Jaffar had been able to break down the first door. As they stood frozen, a gust of wind blew through the tunnel from where the first door had opened, blowing out all the lanterns. All, that is, except the one in Sara's hand.

The girls could hear Jaffar's footsteps falter for a moment, caught in the darkness. Then, too soon, he seemed to adjust to the reduced light. The single lantern, close to the Jannah Jewels, must be what he was focusing on to guide him. His footsteps got louder and louder, closer and closer.

"There's nowhere to go! This time we can't run OR hide!" whispered Jaide.

"Put out the lantern," said Iman.

Sara quickly blew it out. Now, it was completely dark in the tunnel, and the footsteps stopped. The girls held their breaths. Then, after what seemed like five minutes, the footsteps started up again. This time, they seemed that they were going farther away.

"Uhm, girls, I think, I think, I think I'm going to sneeze," said Sara. "Aaaaccchhhooooooooooo!"

"There you are!" called Jaffar, and his footsteps started up again.

"Hidayah come on, come on, come on! We have to get out of here," said Iman.

"Please God, please help us get out of this tunnel," Hidayah focused with her whole heart the best she could. 'Oh Most Merciful!' Sara whispered over and over. As Hidayah looked into the pitch darkness, the face of the old man in the archery store burst into her mind. *"I suggest you untie this knot you are in with... the pure end of an arrow."*

*Let me at least try it!* Hidayah thought to herself. With one hand she searched for a knot in the wooden door; with the other, she pulled out an arrow. Finding a big knot with a thin crack across it, Hidayah placed the arrow's end into the space, and heard a click! The door started to move open.

## 11

## No Escape!

"The door, the secret door is moving open!" cried Sara. "But it's all dark on the other side. Where are we going?"

"We have no choice!" said Iman.

Jaffar came charging towards the door. The girls, now on the other side, pushed against it with all their weight. Jaffar tried to stick his hand around the door to stop it from closing. But the door was too heavy and Jaffar had to move his hand or he would lose it. The door clicked shut.

The Jannah Jewels stood on one side and Jaffar on the other.

"Not, this time Jaffar," said Hidayah.

"Grrrrrrrrr! Arrrgghh!" yelled Jaffar.

Jaffar banged his hands against the door. Out of nowhere, the Jannah Jewels heard the patter of light footsteps.

"Jaffar, just let them go. What does it matter now?"

It was Jasmin.

"We've got the artifact. And you even have your silly wish of being the one who gives it to Father. I don't understand what more you want."

"No," screamed Jaffar. "You are wrong. It's not ambergris, you fool!"

"It is!" Jasmin yelled back. "It's ambergris! That's what they were looking for – I heard them and I intercepted them!"

"Well then, Jasmin, even *they* were wrong. I know for sure it is not ambergris."

"Jaffar! What are you talking about? I had to fight them for this!"

"Well, you wasted your time."

"Jaffar, if you are so sure, then what is it? WHAT

IS IT?"

"All I know is that it's the colour of her scarf. And she sure isn't wearing grey."

Jaffar and Jasmin were already moving back down the tunnel, and now their voices got too faint to hear.

The Jannah Jewels stood silent, processing what they had just heard. "Come on," said Hidayah. "Let's get out of here before they find another way to us."

The girls were in an orange grove, it seemed. They walked briskly beneath the fragrant branches.

Finally, Jaide spoke up. "*Whose* scarf?"

Iman answered quietly but with certainty in her voice. "Hidayah's of course. It was crimson, Hidayah. That's what was in the bottle. I was wrong about ambergris. I pushed for ambergris...Abbas wanted us to not get stuck on one idea...but I was so sure."

"It's not your fault, Iman. Let's look at the bright side. At least now we know what it isn't, and what it is, right?" said Hidayah.

"It's just that we only have an hour left, and we are so far from Yeshua's store now."

The stars were emerging, and from where they stood, the girls could see the city below them, street lamps being lit one by one. The Great Mosque of Cordoba with its big lanterns looked magnificent against the backdrop of the bluish purple sky, touched by a hint of moonlight.

"Can you see that big square from up here? That's where Yeshua's store is."

Iman called out for Spirit, and the white horse game galloping towards them. All four Jewels got on. "Okay, girls, start praying. With any good fortune, we'll be at Yeshua's in about half an hour."

## 12

## Crimson

They reached Yeshua's store just as he was locking the front door.

"Oh, girls! How are you?"

"Sir, please, we need a bottle of crimson. Could we have one? We have no time to explain."

"Oh!"

"Please sir, we need it to finish our mission."

Yeshua smiled obligingly, and turned the key back in the other direction, to open his store again. He went inside and the girls followed.

"Crimson, crimson, crimson. I do hope I have some left. It's a very popular product you know…one of the most popular…hmm, I had a big order from a French merchant the other day. I am not sure now… ah - I think I might be out of it."

A wave of panic and worry came rushing over Hidayah. It took all her strength to push it away with hope in Allah. Time was running out!

"Ah yes!" said Yeshua. "And here you are." He held up a bottle that matched the image on the map. "I feel bad about all that happened today, and that strange girl who stole your bottle. She was quite the little thief…here, take this at no cost, girls. Just be on your way safely now."

"Super!" said Jaide.

"Yes!" said Sara.

"Awesome!" said Iman.

Hidayah almost grabbed the bottle in her haste.

"You take care now, girls. And wish me well on my journey. I am going for a visit to the Holy Land, leaving tomorrow by God's will."

"God be with you!" called the girls.

The girls left the square and headed towards the

outskirts of town, riding Spirit. Now they dismounted, seeing a tree in the distance. With a final burst of energy, they started to run towards it.

By the time they reached their tree, Hidayah's lungs ached. Her heart pounded. Her feet burned.

"Ready, 1, 2, 3, push!"

The tree trunk slid open and down they fell into the dark insides of the tree.

Jaide looked at her watch. It glowed the number: 0:00.

## 13

## Stuck in Time?

The Jannah Jewels held hands and said, "*Bismillah-irRahman-irRahim!*"

Nothing happened.

"*Bismillah-irRahman-irRahim!*" cried the Jannah Jewels.

Still nothing.

"Sensei! Where are you?" cried Hidayah. "We brought you the artifact." It was strange. Sensei was nowhere to be seen.

"Oh no," said Jaide. "Are we really too late?"

The Jannah Jewels stood silently for a few minutes. Hidayah was hoping Sensei would emerge at any moment.

When nothing happened for a few minutes, a great worry and fear started to mount inside Hidayah. It came from the bottom of her stomach and grasped at every muscle. She trembled as she slowly walked over to the clock. The Jewels usually placed the artifact in its position only after first presenting it to Sensei, but Hidayah did not know what else to do except carry on, hoping things would make sense.

Hidayah, with hands shaking, stood in front of the clock. She held it to the 4 o'clock position. The other artifacts had always been pulled, as if magnetically drawn, into position.

"What is happening," asked Iman. "Why isn't it clicking into place?"

"I - I don't know," said Hidayah.

Each of the girls gave it a try, but the bottle with the ornate stopper, crimson powder glistening inside, would not click into place.

The girls sat down scared and confused.

Hidayah fiddled with her compass. Then she got

up.

Hidayah prayed the prayer of need. When she prostrated, she stayed there for a very long time. *You are the closest to your Lord when you prostrate to Him,* Sensei had taught. Iman closed her eyes. Jaide started to recite supplications for guidance. Sara whispered her hopes to God. Time seemed to stand still.

Hidayah stood up slowly, having completed her prayer. The girls could see that she was now serene.

"Girls, this is not the right artifact. You all saw what happened. It's clear. This is not the artifact we were supposed to bring."

"But –" said Jaide.

"Do you remember, Abbas said to not jump to any conclusions? Well, we did that twice. First, we didn't have enough proof that it was ambergris. But we pushed ahead with that assumption. Then, when we heard what Jaffar said, we assumed it was crimson. I think we were so pressed for time by then that we just went to option B – crimson - right away without thinking of option C, D, or E.

Iman nodded and looked down.

"And that was an error. Jewels, I am sorry to say it, but we are really stuck in Spain. We need to go back and find the right artifact," said Hidayah.

"So, we have to go back up there?" asked Sara.

"This is all my fault," said Jaide. "I got too happy being here in Andalus; they always say you should be careful of what you wish for!"

The Jannah Jewels fell silent. A tear dropped from Iman's face. The girls huddled close to comfort her. Iman spoke quietly: "Girls, Sensei said this would be hard...."

Hidayah let her heart absorb Iman's brave reminder. The importance of this mission was becoming clearer. It wasn't just about beating Jaffar or collecting artifacts. Hidayah realized for the first time that the secret in the Golden Clock was very important. It had to be a good secret; and because of how good it was, the Jewels had to be brave enough to deserve it.

"Hidayah! You have been chosen. You will need to lead us!" said Iman.

Hidayah took a deep breath, and then, with a brave heart, whispered "*InshaAllah*!"

*Will the Jannah Jewels find the right artifact? Will Jaffar and Jasmin beat them to it? What if the Jannah Jewels really can never get back home? Find out in the next book, Book Five: Courage in Cordoba.*

## Don't miss the next Jannah Jewels book!

In book five, the Jannah Jewels wake up in Spain once again after being trapped back in time. Will the Jannah Jewels figure out what exactly is the right substance? What is the missing artifact? The Jannah Jewels need you to help solve this big mystery!

Find out more about the fifth book by visiting our website at
**www.JannahJewels.com**

# Glossary

**Alhamdulillahi Rabbil Alameen:** "All praise is due to God" in Arabic. This prayer is said when thankful of something or to show appreciation.

**Allah:** God

**Assalamu'alaykum:** "May the peace of God be with you" in Arabic.

**BismillahirRahmanirRaheem:** "In the name of God, Most Merciful, Most Beneficient" in Arabic. This prayer is said before partaking in something.

**Hijab:** a head-scarf

**InshaAllah:** "If it is God's will" in Arabic. It is said when indicating hope for something to occur in the future.

**Jannah:** heaven, paradise or garden

**Madrasah:** a school

**Maghribi script:** It is one of the cursive forms of the Arabic alphabet that developed in North Africa and later in Andalusia.

**Mosque:** A sacred place of worship for Muslims, also commonly called a masjid.

**Quran:** The last holy scripture of the Muslims.

**Rihla:** The title of Ibn Battuta's travel account, also means, a 'journey' in Arabic.

**SubhanAllah:** "Glory be to God" in Arabic. This prayer is said when in awe of something.

**Walaikum asalaam:** "May the peace of God be upon you too" in Arabic

HIDAYAH

JAIDE

To find out more about our other books,

go to:

**www.JannahJewels.com**

Made in the USA
San Bernardino, CA
30 April 2017